# EXPOSING FAMILY COURT CORRUPTION IN CONNECTICUT: A SYSTEM BETRAYED

*by Margaret Sullivan & Joy Winters*

# Exposing Family Court Corruption in Connecticut: A System Betrayed

This book is for informational purposes only. The authors are not legal professionals but have been through the family court system and researched the content extensively. If you need legal advice consult with a licensed attorney.

# DEDICATION

This book is dedicated to Bean and Bud, my favorite children in the whole wide world. I am deeply sorry for the pain and emotional trauma caused by Judge Albis and your father when they took you away from me. Every day, I have been fighting to have you back in my life.

On August 14, 2024, the Connecticut Supreme Court ruled that Judge Albis and your father were wrong. Judge Albis had ordered that visitation with me would be determined by your father, who could even suspend visitation with Bud. Arguing pro se, I was able to reverse that decision.

I am truly sorry that we had to be separated for so long—it should have never happened. Our experience is a stark example of the corruption in the Connecticut family court system, which often separates loving parents from their children. What happened to us cannot happen again, and in a way, Bean and Bud, you have also been a part of changing the law and helping to reform family court.

Luv luvs,
Mom-ly

# TABLE OF CONTENTS

# Introduction

## Overview of Family Courts

Family courts are designed to be sanctuaries of justice and fairness, tasked with some of the most delicate and impactful responsibilities in the judicial system. These courts handle cases involving divorce, child custody, alimony, child support, and other family-related legal matters. The decisions made within these walls shape the futures of families, protect the well-being of children, and ensure that the rights of all parties are fairly represented and respected.

# The Importance of Family Courts

In an ideal world, family courts would function flawlessly, ensuring that justice prevails and that all parties receive fair treatment. These courts are essential to maintaining social order and stability by resolving conflicts that could otherwise escalate into more serious societal issues. When functioning properly, family courts provide a critical service, offering resolutions that are in the best interests of children and families.

# Introducing the Problem

However, the reality within many family courts, including those in Connecticut, is far from this ideal. Corruption, bias, and inefficiency can infiltrate the system, leading to unjust outcomes that can devastate families. This book aims to shine a light on the darker side of family courts in

Connecticut, exposing the corruption that can undermine the very principles of justice these courts are meant to uphold.

## The Scope of Corruption

Corruption in family courts can take many forms, from blatant bribery and favoritism to more subtle forms of bias and incompetence. Judges, lawyers, and other court officials may act out of self-interest, be influenced by personal biases, or simply lack the necessary training and resources to handle complex family law cases effectively. These issues can lead to unjust rulings, prolonged legal battles, and immense emotional and financial strain on families.

## The Impact on Families

For those who become entangled in a corrupt family court system, the consequences can be devastating. Children may be placed in harmful environments, parents may be unfairly deprived of custody, and families can be financially ruined by the cost of ongoing legal disputes. The emotional toll on parents and children alike can be profound, leading to long-term psychological harm and strained family relationships.

## The Need for Reform

Addressing corruption in Connecticut's family courts is not just a matter of individual justice but a societal imperative. It requires comprehensive reform efforts, increased oversight, and a commitment to transparency and accountability. By exposing the issues and advocating for change, we can work towards a family court system that truly serves the best interests of all parties involved.

## Purpose of This Book

This book is intended to serve as a wake-up call and a call to action. Through detailed analysis, real-life case studies, and personal stories from those affected, it aims to shed light on the extent of the problem in Connecticut and to offer practical solutions for reform. By doing so, we hope to inspire individuals, advocacy groups, and policymakers to join the fight for a fairer, more just family court system.

## Acknowledgements

We extend our gratitude to the many individuals and organizations who have contributed their time, expertise, and personal stories to this book. Their courage and commitment to justice are the driving forces behind this effort.

# Call to Action

As you read through the pages of this book, we encourage you to reflect on the importance of fair and just family courts. Consider how you can contribute to the movement for reform, whether through advocacy, support for affected families, or by spreading awareness of the issues at hand. Together, we can work towards a system that truly embodies the principles of justice and fairness for all families in Connecticut.

# Chapter 1: Understanding Family Court in Connecticut

## History of Connecticut Family Courts

The family court system in Connecticut has a rich history that reflects the evolution of family law in the United States. Originally, family-related legal matters were handled by various courts, including probate and common pleas courts. It wasn't until the mid-20th century that Connecticut, like many other states, recognized the need for a specialized court system to handle the increasing complexities of family law.

The establishment of family courts was driven by the need for a more focused and specialized approach to cases involving divorce, child custody, alimony, and other family matters. The goal was to create a court system that was not only knowledgeable about family law but also sensitive to the emotional and psychological aspects of family disputes. This specialization aimed to provide more consistent and fair rulings, ultimately benefiting the families involved.

# Key Legislative Milestones

Several key legislative milestones have shaped the Connecticut family court system:

1. **Uniform Marriage and Divorce Act (1970):** This act aimed to standardize marriage and divorce laws across the United States.

Connecticut adopted several provisions, leading to more uniformity and predictability in divorce proceedings.

2. **Connecticut Family Court Act (1973):** This act officially established the family court system in Connecticut, providing a separate judicial framework for handling family law cases.

3. **Child Support Enforcement Amendments (1984):** These amendments strengthened the enforcement of child support orders, ensuring that non-custodial parents met their financial obligations.

4. **Domestic Violence Prevention and Services Act (1994):** This act provided increased protections for victims of domestic violence, including access to restraining orders and other legal remedies.

5. **Revisions to the Connecticut Child Custody Laws (2005):** These revisions emphasized the best interests of the child in custody determinations, promoting joint custody arrangements and the involvement of both parents.

6. Requirement to Develop Guardian Ad Litem Guidelines (2011): The law failed to address the needs of children, instead required the establishment of guidelines by 2012 by the judicial community.  It allows for quasi-judicial immunity and fails to include accountability, supervisory, or practice requirements.

7. Jennifer's Law (2021) expanded the definition of domestic violence to include coercive control.  While the law was intended to help women receive

additional protections, men have been successful weaponizing the law against the women it was meant to protect. While the law is a good starting point and much like the best interests of the child standards, it needs revision. Training for judicial authorities and police officers is necessary for them to understand the criteria and characteristics of coercive control, ensuring they are able to protect the safety of victims.

## Structure and Function

Connecticut's family court system is designed to handle a wide range of cases, each requiring specialized knowledge and sensitivity. The structure and function of these courts are as follows:

# Roles of Judges

Family court judges in Connecticut are responsible for presiding over cases involving divorce, child custody, alimony, child support, domestic violence, and more. These judges are expected to have a deep understanding of family law and to approach each case with impartiality and empathy. Their rulings can have profound and lasting impacts on the lives of families, making their role both critical and challenging.

# Roles of Lawyers

Lawyers play a crucial role in the family court system. They represent the interests of their clients, whether they are seeking a divorce, custody of their children, or protection from domestic violence. Lawyers must navigate the complexities of family law, advocate for their clients' rights, and strive to achieve the best possible outcomes. In

Connecticut, family law attorneys are often specialized in this area, bringing expertise and experience to their cases.

## Other Court Officials

In addition to judges and lawyers, several other court officials contribute to the functioning of family courts in Connecticut:

- **Family Relations Counselors:** These professionals assist the court by conducting evaluations and making recommendations regarding child custody and visitation arrangements.
- **Guardians ad Litem (GAL):** Appointed by the court, GALs represent the best interests of the child in custody disputes.
- **Court Clerks:** They manage the administrative aspects of court proceedings, ensuring that cases are processed efficiently and that

all necessary documentation is
filed.

# Typical Cases Handled
by Connecticut Family
Courts

Family courts in Connecticut handle a
variety of cases, each with its own
unique challenges and requirements:

## Divorce

Divorce cases are among the most
common in family courts. They involve
the legal dissolution of a marriage and
often include issues related to the
division of assets, alimony, and child
custody. In Connecticut, divorces can be
contested or uncontested, with
contested cases typically requiring more
extensive legal proceedings.

## Child Custody

Child custody cases determine the
living arrangements and parental

responsibilities for children following a divorce or separation. Connecticut family courts prioritize the best interests of the child, considering factors such as the child's age, health, emotional ties to each parent, and the parents' ability to provide a stable environment.

## Child Support

Child support cases involve the financial responsibilities of non-custodial parents towards their children. The courts use specific guidelines to calculate child support payments, ensuring that the child's needs are met while balancing the financial capabilities of both parents.

## Alimony

Alimony, or spousal support, is another common issue in family courts. It involves one spouse providing financial support to the other following a divorce. The court considers factors such as the length of the marriage, the financial status of each spouse, and the standard of living during the marriage when determining alimony awards.

## Domestic Violence

Family courts also handle cases of domestic violence, providing legal protections for victims. This can include restraining orders, custody determinations, and other measures to ensure the safety of those affected by domestic abuse.

# Conclusion

Understanding the structure, function, and history of family courts in Connecticut is essential to grasp the complexities and challenges inherent in this judicial system. While these courts are designed to provide justice and protect the interests of families, the presence of corruption and bias can undermine these goals. As we delve deeper into the issues plaguing

Connecticut's family courts, it becomes clear that reform and vigilance are necessary to uphold the principles of fairness and justice that these courts were established to protect.

# CHAPTER 2: IDENTIFYING CORRUPTION

## Definition of Corruption in Family Courts

Corruption in family courts can be broadly defined as the abuse of power by court officials for personal gain or to serve biased interests, leading to unjust outcomes. This corruption can manifest in various forms, including bribery, favoritism, bias, incompetence, and procedural irregularities. In Connecticut, as in other states, such corruption undermines the integrity of the judicial system and erodes public trust.

# Forms of Corruption

## Bribery

Bribery involves court officials accepting money or other favors in exchange for favorable rulings. This practice is illegal and unethical, yet it persists in some instances, often hidden from public scrutiny. In family courts, bribery can lead to unjust decisions in divorce settlements, custody arrangements, and alimony awards.

## Favoritism

Favoritism occurs when judges or other court officials show preferential treatment to certain parties based on personal relationships, social connections, or biases. This can result in one party receiving more favorable outcomes regardless of the legal merits of the case.

## Bias

Bias in family courts can stem from personal prejudices of judges or other court officials. This can include biases based on gender, race, socioeconomic status, or other factors. Bias can significantly influence the outcome of cases, leading to unfair treatment of one party over another.

## Incompetence

Incompetence involves court officials lacking the necessary knowledge, skills, or training to handle family law cases effectively. This can lead to poorly reasoned decisions, mishandling of evidence, and other procedural errors that adversely affect the fairness of the proceedings.

## Procedural Irregularities

Procedural irregularities refer to deviations from established legal processes and protocols. These can include improper handling of evidence, failure to follow due process, and other violations of court rules. Such irregularities can undermine the fairness and integrity of the judicial process.

# Impact on Justice and Families

The impact of corruption in family courts is profound, affecting both the judicial system and the families involved. Corruption can lead to unjust rulings, prolonged legal battles, and immense emotional and financial strain on families. When justice is compromised, it undermines public confidence in the legal system and perpetuates a cycle of injustice.

## Emotional and Psychological Effects

The emotional and psychological toll on families involved in corrupt family court proceedings can be devastating. Children may be placed in harmful environments, parents may be unfairly deprived of custody, and the stress of prolonged legal battles can lead to long-term psychological harm.

## Financial Consequences

Corruption can also have significant financial consequences for families. Prolonged legal battles drain financial resources, and unjust rulings can result in unfair financial obligations. The economic strain can be overwhelming, leading to financial instability and hardship.

# Case Studies

## Case Study 1: The Smith Family

In one notable case in Connecticut, the Smith family experienced the devastating effects of judicial corruption. During their custody battle, evidence surfaced that the judge had accepted bribes from one party. As a result, the court awarded custody to an unfit parent, leading to severe emotional and psychological harm for the children involved. The case garnered public attention, highlighting the need for greater oversight and accountability in family courts.

## Case Study 2: The Johnson Divorce

The Johnson divorce case involved allegations of favoritism and bias. The judge handling the case had a personal relationship with one of the lawyers, leading to a series of rulings that favored that lawyer's client. Despite clear evidence supporting the other party's claims, the court consistently ruled against them, resulting in an unjust division of assets and custody arrangement. The Johnson case underscored the detrimental effects of personal biases and the importance of impartiality in the judiciary.

## Analysis of How These Cases Were Handled

In both case studies, the handling of the cases revealed significant flaws in the system. The lack of oversight allowed corrupt practices to go unchecked, and the affected families had limited recourse to challenge the unjust rulings. These cases illustrate the urgent need for reforms to address corruption and ensure fairness in family court proceedings.

## Conclusion

Identifying and understanding the various forms of corruption in Connecticut's family courts is the first step toward addressing and rectifying these issues. The impact of corruption is far-reaching, affecting not only the immediate families involved but also the broader public trust in the judicial system. Through detailed case studies and analysis, it becomes clear that systemic changes are necessary to combat corruption and uphold the principles of justice and fairness that family courts are meant to protect. As we move forward, it is essential to advocate for increased transparency, accountability, and oversight to restore integrity to the family court system in Connecticut.

# Chapter 3: Causes of Corruption

## Systemic Issues in Connecticut

Corruption in Connecticut's family courts, like in many judicial systems, is often rooted in systemic issues that create an environment where unethical behavior can thrive. Addressing these systemic issues is crucial for understanding and combating corruption.

## Lack of Oversight and Accountability

One of the primary systemic issues is the lack of effective oversight and accountability mechanisms. Family court judges and officials often operate with a high degree of autonomy, making it difficult to monitor their actions and hold them accountable for unethical behavior. The absence of regular, independent audits and evaluations allows corrupt practices to go undetected and unaddressed.

## Inadequate Training and Resources

Family law is complex and requires specialized knowledge and skills. However, many judges and court officials in Connecticut may lack adequate training in this area. Inadequate training can lead to incompetence, which, in turn, can contribute to corruption as officials rely on improper shortcuts or biased judgments due to a lack of understanding. Additionally, family courts often operate with limited resources, further straining the system and increasing the likelihood of errors and misconduct.

## Procedural Inefficiencies

The procedural inefficiencies within Connecticut's family courts can also contribute to corruption. Delays, backlogs, and cumbersome processes can frustrate both court officials and litigants, leading to a desire for quick, albeit improper, resolutions. These inefficiencies can create opportunities for bribery and favoritism, as parties may be willing to pay for expedited or favorable outcomes.

## Individual Factors

While systemic issues provide the backdrop for corruption, individual factors play a significant role in perpetuating unethical behavior within family courts. Understanding these factors is essential for addressing the root causes of corruption.

# Personal Biases and Conflicts of Interest

Judges and court officials are human and can be influenced by personal biases and conflicts of interest. These biases can stem from personal beliefs, past experiences, or relationships with parties involved in the case. Conflicts of interest, where court officials have personal or financial stakes in the outcome, can also compromise their impartiality. These factors can lead to decisions that are not based on legal merits but on personal inclinations.

# Financial Incentives and Pressures

Financial incentives and pressures are powerful motivators for corruption. Family court cases often involve significant financial stakes, including property division, alimony, and child support. Court officials may succumb to bribery or other forms of corruption due to financial pressures or the allure of financial gain. This can lead to decisions that favor the party offering the bribe, regardless of the case's merits.

# The Role of Attorneys and Guardians ad Litem

Attorneys and guardians ad litem (GALs) play crucial roles in family court proceedings, and their actions can either contribute to or help combat corruption. Understanding their influence is key to addressing the problem.

## Attorneys

Attorneys represent their clients' interests and are expected to adhere to ethical standards. However, some attorneys may engage in unethical practices, such as bribing court officials or exploiting procedural loopholes, to secure favorable outcomes for their clients. These actions can perpetuate corruption within the system and undermine the integrity of the judicial process.

## Guardians ad Litem

Guardians ad litem are appointed to represent the best interests of children in custody disputes. While their role is intended to be neutral and focused on the child's welfare, GALs can sometimes be influenced by biases, personal relationships, or financial incentives. When GALs act unethically, they can contribute to unjust outcomes and exacerbate the impact of corruption on families.

# Cultural and Social Factors

Cultural and social factors within Connecticut can also contribute to corruption in family courts. Understanding these factors can provide insights into the broader context in which corruption occurs.

## Societal Attitudes

Societal attitudes towards family roles, gender, and authority can influence the behavior of court officials and the outcomes of cases. For example, traditional views on gender roles can lead to biased decisions in custody and alimony cases. Additionally, societal acceptance of certain unethical behaviors, such as bribery, can normalize corruption and make it more difficult to combat.

## Public Awareness and Advocacy

Public awareness and advocacy play crucial roles in addressing corruption. A lack of awareness about the prevalence and impact of corruption in family courts can allow unethical practices to continue unchecked. Conversely, strong advocacy efforts and public pressure can drive reforms and increase accountability within the system.

# Conclusion

The causes of corruption in Connecticut's family courts are multifaceted, involving systemic issues, individual factors, and broader cultural and social influences. Addressing these root causes requires a comprehensive approach that includes improving oversight and accountability, enhancing training and resources, addressing personal biases and financial pressures, and fostering public awareness and advocacy. By tackling these underlying issues, we can work towards creating a family court system that upholds the principles of justice and fairness for all families in Connecticut.

# Chapter 4: The Impact on Families

## Emotional and Psychological Effects

Corruption in family courts can have profound emotional and psychological effects on all parties involved, particularly children. The stress and trauma resulting from unjust court rulings and prolonged legal battles can lead to long-lasting psychological harm.

## Stress and Trauma on Children

Children are often the most vulnerable in family court proceedings. When corruption leads to unjust custody decisions, children may be placed in harmful or unstable environments. The emotional turmoil from being separated from a parent or forced to live in a contentious situation can manifest in various ways:

- **Anxiety and Depression:** Children exposed to prolonged conflict and instability may develop anxiety and depression, affecting their overall well-being and development.
- **Behavioral Issues:** Stress and trauma can lead to behavioral problems, including aggression, withdrawal, and difficulties in school.
- **Trust Issues:** Experiencing or witnessing injustice in the court system can lead to a loss of trust in authority figures and institutions, impacting a child's future relationships and interactions.

# Emotional Toll on Parents

For parents, the emotional toll of corruption in family courts can be overwhelming. Unjust rulings can lead to feelings of helplessness, anger, and despair. Parents may experience:

- **Depression and Anxiety:** The stress of fighting a corrupt system can lead to mental health issues, impacting their ability to function effectively in daily life and as a parent.
- **Parental Alienation:** When a parent is unjustly deprived of custody or visitation, it can lead to alienation from their children, causing profound grief and loss.
- **Strained Relationships:** The emotional strain can also affect relationships with new partners, extended family, and friends, leading to isolation and further emotional distress.

# Financial Consequences

The financial impact of corruption in family courts is significant, often exacerbating the emotional and psychological effects.

# Cost of Prolonged Legal Battles

Corruption can lead to prolonged legal battles as parties seek to challenge unjust rulings. This can result in:

- **Legal Fees:** Continuous legal representation and court fees can quickly accumulate, draining financial resources.
- **Lost Income:** Time spent in court or dealing with legal issues can result in lost work hours and reduced income, further straining financial stability.
- **Debt:** The financial burden can force families into debt, affecting their long-term economic

prospects and overall quality of life.

# Unfair Financial Obligations

Unjust rulings can also lead to unfair financial obligations, such as:

- **Excessive Alimony and Child Support:** Biased or corrupt decisions may result in one party being required to pay excessive amounts, creating financial hardship.
- **Unjust Property Division:** Corruption can lead to inequitable division of assets, leaving one party at a significant financial disadvantage.

# Long-term Consequences on Family Dynamics

The impact of corruption in family courts extends beyond immediate emotional and financial effects, influencing long-term family dynamics and relationships.

## Strained Parent-Child Relationships

Unjust rulings can lead to strained relationships between parents and children. Children may struggle to understand the reasons behind court decisions, leading to confusion and resentment. Over time, this can create deep-seated issues that affect the parent-child bond.

## Intergenerational Effects

The trauma and financial instability caused by corrupt court decisions can have intergenerational effects. Children who experience significant stress and instability are more likely to face challenges in their own adult relationships and parenting. The cycle of trauma and instability can thus continue across generations.

# Case Studies

## Case Study 1: The Martinez Family

The Martinez family faced a corrupt family court system when seeking custody of their children. Despite clear evidence of the father's abusive behavior, the court awarded him primary custody due to bribery. The children were subjected to a harmful environment, leading to severe emotional and psychological distress. The mother's attempts to fight the ruling resulted in financial ruin and profound emotional trauma.

## Case Study 2: The Davis Divorce

In the Davis divorce case, the wife was unfairly favored by the court due to her lawyer's connections with the judge. The husband was left with minimal visitation rights and excessive financial obligations, despite evidence that a more balanced arrangement was in the children's best interests. This led to financial instability and strained relationships between the father and his children, who struggled to understand the court's decisions.

## Conclusion

The impact of corruption in Connecticut's family courts on families is profound and multifaceted. The emotional and psychological toll, coupled with significant financial consequences, can devastate families, leaving long-lasting scars. The case studies illustrate the human cost of corruption, highlighting the urgent need for systemic reforms to protect families and ensure justice. By addressing these issues, we can work towards a family court system that truly serves the best interests of children and families, fostering stability and fairness.

# CHAPTER 5: LEGAL AND ETHICAL VIOLATIONS

## Overview of Legal Violations

Corruption in family courts often involves a range of legal violations that undermine the judicial system's integrity. These violations can take various forms, each contributing to unjust outcomes and eroding public trust in the legal system.

## Bribery and Fraud

Bribery and fraud are among the most egregious legal violations in family courts. Bribery occurs when judges, lawyers, or other court officials accept money or favors in exchange for favorable rulings. Fraud involves the intentional deception of the court to secure unjust outcomes. Both practices are illegal and can lead to criminal charges, but they can be difficult to detect and prove.

- **Example:** A judge accepting a bribe from one party to award custody to an unfit parent, despite evidence to the contrary.
- **Legal Consequences:** Bribery and fraud can result in criminal charges, including imprisonment, fines, and disbarment for legal professionals.

## Conflict of Interest

A conflict of interest occurs when a court official has a personal or financial interest in the outcome of a case. This can lead to biased decisions that do not reflect the case's merits. Conflicts of interest are unethical and can violate legal standards of impartiality and fairness.

- **Example:** A judge presiding over a case involving a close friend or relative, leading to biased rulings.
- **Legal Consequences:** Conflicts of interest can result in recusal of the judge, overturning of decisions, and disciplinary actions against the involved parties.

## Procedural Violations

Procedural violations involve deviations from established legal processes and protocols. These violations can include improper handling of evidence, failure to follow due process, and other procedural errors that compromise the fairness of court proceedings.

- **Example:** Ignoring evidence presented by one party or failing to adhere to required timelines for hearings and decisions.

- **Legal Consequences:** Procedural violations can lead to appeals, reversals of court decisions, and disciplinary actions against court officials.

## Ethical Violations

Ethical violations in family courts often go hand-in-hand with legal violations, as unethical behavior undermines the principles of justice and fairness. These violations can be perpetrated by judges, lawyers, and other court officials, contributing to a culture of corruption.

## Bias and Prejudice

Bias and prejudice involve judges or court officials allowing their personal beliefs or prejudices to influence their decisions. This can result in unfair treatment of one party based on gender, race, socioeconomic status, or other factors.

- **Example:** A judge consistently ruling against fathers in custody cases due to personal beliefs about gender roles.
- **Ethical Consequences:** Bias and prejudice can lead to complaints, disciplinary actions, and loss of judicial or legal licenses.

## Lack of Transparency

A lack of transparency in court proceedings can foster corruption and prevent accountability. Transparency involves clear, open, and accessible court processes that allow for public scrutiny and ensure that decisions are based on the law and evidence.

- **Example:** Sealing court records without valid legal reasons or conducting hearings behind closed doors.
- **Ethical Consequences:** Lack of transparency can result in public distrust, calls for judicial reform,

and potential disciplinary
actions.

## Incompetence

Incompetence occurs when court
officials lack the necessary knowledge,
skills, or diligence to handle family law
cases effectively. This can lead to poorly
reasoned decisions and mishandling of
cases, contributing to unjust outcomes.

- **Example:** A judge failing to
  understand the nuances of child
  psychology when making
  custody decisions.
- **Ethical Consequences:**
  Incompetence can lead to
  mandatory training, suspension,
  or removal from the bench or
  legal practice.

# Regulatory and Oversight Mechanisms

To combat legal and ethical violations, effective regulatory and oversight mechanisms are essential. These mechanisms help ensure that family court officials adhere to legal standards and ethical principles.

# Judicial Review and Appeals

Judicial review and appeals processes allow higher courts to review and overturn decisions made by lower courts. This provides a crucial check on potential corruption and ensures that errors and injustices can be corrected.

- **Example:** An appellate court reviewing a custody decision influenced by bribery and overturning the ruling.
- **Impact:** Judicial review and appeals help maintain the

integrity of the judicial system by providing avenues for redress and correction.

## Judicial Conduct Commissions

Judicial conduct commissions are independent bodies responsible for investigating and addressing complaints against judges. These commissions can impose sanctions, recommend removal, and enforce ethical standards.

- **Example:** A judicial conduct commission investigating allegations of bias and imposing disciplinary actions against a judge.
- **Impact:** Judicial conduct commissions help ensure accountability and uphold ethical standards within the judiciary.

## Legal Bar Associations

Legal bar associations play a vital role in regulating the conduct of lawyers. They enforce ethical standards, investigate complaints, and can disbar attorneys who engage in unethical behavior.

- **Example:** A bar association disbarring a lawyer found guilty of bribery and fraud.
- **Impact:** Legal bar associations help maintain the integrity of the legal profession by holding attorneys accountable for their actions.

## Conclusion

Legal and ethical violations in Connecticut's family courts have severe consequences for justice and public trust. Understanding these violations and the mechanisms in place to address them is crucial for combating corruption and ensuring fairness. By strengthening regulatory and oversight mechanisms, enhancing transparency, and promoting accountability, we can work towards a family court system that upholds the principles of justice and serves the best interests of families.

# Chapter 6: Family Court Corruption and Narcissistic Abuse in Connecticut

## Introduction

Family courts are designed to resolve disputes and ensure the well-being of children and vulnerable family members. However, when corruption infiltrates the system, it can lead to unjust outcomes, particularly in cases involving narcissistic abuse.

Narcissistic abusers, skilled at manipulation and deception, often exploit weaknesses in the family court system, further victimizing their targets. This chapter explores the intersection of family court corruption and narcissistic abuse in Connecticut, highlighting the challenges victims face and advocating for systemic reforms.

## Understanding Narcissistic Abuse

Narcissistic abuse is a form of emotional and psychological manipulation perpetrated by individuals with narcissistic personality traits. Narcissists often exhibit:

**Grandiosity and Entitlement**: A sense of superiority and belief that they are entitled to special treatment.

**Lack of Empathy**: Inability to recognize or care about the feelings and needs of others.

**Manipulation and Control**: Using deceit, charm, and coercion to dominate and control others.

**Gaslighting**: Making the victim doubt their reality and sanity. In the context of family court, these behaviors can make it exceedingly difficult for victims to present their case effectively and obtain justice.

# The Role of Family Court Corruption

Family court corruption exacerbates the difficulties faced by victims of narcissistic abuse. Corruption can take several forms:

**Judicial Bias and Misconduct**: Judges may exhibit bias due to personal prejudices, lack of understanding of narcissistic abuse, or even financial incentives.

**Ineffective Legal Representation**:
Lawyers may fail to advocate
adequately for their clients, sometimes
due to conflicts of interest or
incompetence.

**Influence of Narcissistic Abusers**:
Narcissists are often adept at charming
and manipulating court officials,
presenting a misleadingly positive
image of themselves while discrediting
their victims.

**Lack of Accountability**: Insufficient
oversight and accountability
mechanisms allow corruption and bias
to persist unchecked.

# Case Studies: The Impact on Victims
## Case Study 1: The Story of Lisa
Lisa, a Connecticut mother, found
herself entangled in a bitter custody

battle with her narcissistic ex-husband. Despite substantial evidence of emotional abuse, the court awarded joint custody, influenced by the ex-husband's charismatic demeanor and strategic manipulation. Lisa's pleas for sole custody to protect her children were dismissed, and she continues to face ongoing harassment and control.

## Case Study 2: The Story of David

David, another victim of narcissistic abuse, struggled to convince the court of his ex-wife's manipulative and harmful behavior. The court-appointed Guardian ad Litem (GAL) sided with his ex-wife, failing to recognize the subtle but pervasive abuse. As a result, David lost significant parenting time, and his relationship with his children suffered.

These case studies illustrate the profound impact of family court corruption on victims of narcissistic abuse, highlighting the urgent need for reform. Legislative Efforts and Advocacy Connecticut has made strides in addressing issues within the family court system, including the introduction of Jennifer's Law, which broadens the definition of domestic violence to include coercive control. However, more targeted efforts are needed to combat narcissistic abuse and family court corruption.

# Key Legislative and Advocacy Measures Training for Judges and Court Officials:

Comprehensive training on recognizing and understanding narcissistic abuse is essential. Judges, GALs, and other court officials must be educated about the tactics used by narcissistic abusers and the profound impact on victims.

# Enhanced Protective Measures:

Laws should be strengthened to provide better protection for victims, including more stringent criteria for granting custody and visitation rights in cases involving allegations of narcissistic abuse.

# Transparency and Accountability:

Implementing mechanisms to ensure transparency in family court proceedings and holding court officials accountable for misconduct is crucial. Support Services for Victims: Providing resources such as legal aid, counseling, and advocacy for victims can help them navigate the complex and often hostile family court environment.

# The Path Forward

Reforming the family court system to better address narcissistic abuse and corruption requires a multifaceted approach. Key steps include:

## Public Awareness and Education:

Raising awareness about narcissistic abuse and the challenges within the family court system can mobilize public support for reform.

## Collaboration with Advocacy Groups:

Partnering with organizations dedicated to family court reform and domestic violence prevention can amplify efforts to create meaningful change.

## Continuous Legislative Advocacy:

Advocating for ongoing legislative changes to protect victims and ensure fair and just family court proceedings is essential.

## Conclusion

Family court corruption and narcissistic abuse are deeply intertwined issues that demand urgent attention and action. By recognizing the unique challenges posed by narcissistic abusers and addressing systemic corruption within the family court system, Connecticut can move towards a more just and equitable future for all families.

Ensuring that victims of narcissistic abuse receive the protection and justice they deserve is not only a moral imperative but also a necessary step in upholding the integrity of our legal system.

Advocacy for these changes can help create a family court system that better

protects the emotional and
psychological health of children.

# Chapter 7: Family Court Corruption and Narcissistic Abuse in Connecticut

## Introduction

Family courts are designed to resolve disputes and ensure the well-being of children and vulnerable family members. However, when corruption infiltrates the system, it can lead to unjust outcomes, particularly in cases involving narcissistic abuse. Narcissistic abusers, skilled at manipulation and deception, often exploit weaknesses in the family court system, further victimizing their targets. This chapter explores the intersection of family court corruption and narcissistic abuse in Connecticut, highlighting the challenges victims face and advocating for systemic reforms.

## Understanding Narcissistic Abuse

Narcissistic abuse is a form of emotional and psychological manipulation perpetrated by individuals with narcissistic personality traits. Narcissists often exhibit:

**Grandiosity and Entitlement**: A sense of superiority and belief that they are entitled to special treatment.

**Lack of Empathy**: Inability to recognize or care about the feelings and needs of others.

**Manipulation and Control**: Using deceit, charm, and coercion to dominate and control others.

**Gaslighting**: Making the victim doubt their reality and sanity.

In the context of family court, these behaviors can make it exceedingly difficult for victims to present their case effectively and obtain justice.

# The Role of Family Court Corruption

Family court corruption exacerbates the difficulties faced by victims of narcissistic abuse. Corruption can take several forms:

**Judicial Bias and Misconduct**: Judges may exhibit bias due to personal prejudices, lack of understanding of narcissistic abuse, or even financial incentives.

**Ineffective Legal Representation**: Lawyers may fail to advocate adequately for their clients, sometimes due to conflicts of interest or incompetence.

**Influence of Narcissistic Abusers**: Narcissists are often adept at charming and manipulating court officials, presenting a misleadingly positive image of themselves while discrediting their victims.

**Lack of Accountability**: Insufficient oversight and accountability mechanisms allow corruption and bias to persist unchecked.

# Case Studies: The Impact on Victims

## Case Study 1: The Story of Lisa

Lisa, a Connecticut mother, found herself entangled in a bitter custody battle with her narcissistic ex-husband. Despite substantial evidence of emotional abuse, the court awarded joint custody, influenced by the ex-husband's charismatic demeanor and strategic manipulation. Lisa's pleas for sole custody to protect her children were dismissed, and she continues to face ongoing harassment and control.

## Case Study 2: The Story of David

David, another victim of narcissistic abuse, struggled to convince the court of his ex-wife's manipulative and harmful behavior. The court-appointed Guardian ad Litem (GAL) sided with his ex-wife, failing to recognize the subtle but pervasive abuse. As a result, David lost significant parenting time, and his relationship with his children suffered.

These case studies illustrate the profound impact of family court corruption on victims of narcissistic abuse, highlighting the urgent need for reform. Legislative Efforts and Advocacy Connecticut has made strides in addressing issues within the family court system, including the introduction of Jennifer's Law, which broadens the definition of domestic violence to include coercive control. However, more targeted efforts are needed to combat narcissistic abuse and family court corruption.

## Key Legislative and Advocacy Measures Training for Judges and Court Officials:

Comprehensive training on recognizing and understanding narcissistic abuse is essential. Judges, GALs, and other court officials must be educated about the tactics used by narcissistic abusers and the profound impact on victims.

## Enhanced Protective Measures:

Laws should be strengthened to provide better protection for victims, including more stringent criteria for granting custody and visitation rights in cases involving allegations of narcissistic abuse.

## Transparency and Accountability:

Implementing mechanisms to ensure transparency in family court proceedings and holding court officials accountable for misconduct is crucial.

## Support Services for Victims:

Providing resources such as legal aid, counseling, and advocacy for victims can help them navigate the complex and often hostile family court environment.

## The Path Forward

Reforming the family court system to better address narcissistic abuse and corruption requires a multifaceted approach. Key steps include:

## Public Awareness and Education:

Raising awareness about narcissistic abuse and the challenges within the family court system can mobilize public support for reform.

## Collaboration with Advocacy Groups:

Partnering with organizations dedicated to family court reform and domestic violence prevention can amplify efforts to create meaningful change.

## Continuous Legislative Advocacy:

Advocating for ongoing legislative changes to protect victims and ensure

fair and just family court proceedings is
essential.

## Conclusion

Family court corruption and narcissistic
abuse are deeply intertwined issues that
demand urgent attention and action. By
recognizing the unique challenges
posed by narcissistic abusers and
addressing systemic corruption within
the family court system, Connecticut
can move towards a more just and
equitable future for all families.

Ensuring that victims of narcissistic
abuse receive the protection and justice
they deserve is not only a moral
imperative but also a necessary step in
upholding the integrity of our legal
system.

Advocacy for these changes can help
create a family court system that better
protects the emotional and
psychological health of children.

# Chapter 8: Jennifer's Law

## Introduction

In recent years, there has been growing recognition of the impact of coercive control in abusive relationships and the limitations of traditional legal frameworks in addressing this insidious form of abuse. Jennifer's Law, named in honor of Jennifer Farber Dulos and Jennifer Magnano, both victims of domestic violence, represents a significant step forward in addressing these issues. This chapter explores Jennifer's Law, the concept of coercive control, and the need for comprehensive family court reform to protect victims and ensure justice.

# Jennifer's Law: A New Paradigm in Addressing Domestic Violence

Jennifer's Law was enacted in Connecticut in 2021, expanding the legal definition of domestic violence to include coercive control. This legislation acknowledges that domestic violence is not always physical but can encompass a range of behaviors designed to dominate and control the victim. Coercive control includes psychological, emotional, financial, and technological abuse, which can be just as damaging as physical violence.

# Coercive Control: Understanding the Dynamics of Abuse

Coercive control is a pattern of behavior used by abusers to instill fear and compliance in their victims. Unlike physical abuse, which often leaves visible scars, coercive control operates through manipulation, isolation, and intimidation. Abusers may restrict their victim's access to money, monitor their communications, control their movements, and undermine their self-esteem. This form of abuse can trap victims in a state of perpetual fear and helplessness, making it incredibly difficult for them to escape the abusive relationship.

## Challenges in Recognizing and Proving Coercive Control

One of the primary challenges in addressing coercive control is its invisibility. Traditional legal systems are often ill-equipped to recognize non-physical forms of abuse. Victims may struggle to provide concrete evidence of coercive control, and law enforcement and the courts may lack the training to identify and respond to these behaviors appropriately. Jennifer's Law aims to bridge this gap by providing a legal framework for recognizing and addressing coercive control, but there is still much work to be done to ensure its effective implementation.

## Family Court Reform: Addressing the Needs of Victims

Family courts play a crucial role in adjudicating cases of domestic violence and child custody. However, these courts have historically been criticized for their handling of such cases, often prioritizing parental rights over the safety and well-being of victims and children. To address these concerns, comprehensive family court reform is necessary. Key Elements of Family

Court Reform Training and Education: Judges, attorneys, and court personnel must receive specialized training on coercive control and the dynamics of domestic violence. This training should include how to recognize non-physical forms of abuse and understand the long-term impacts on victims and children.

## Protective Measures:

Courts should prioritize the safety of victims and children by implementing protective measures, such as emergency restraining orders and supervised visitation. These measures can help prevent further abuse and provide a safer environment for victims to rebuild their lives.

## Holistic Support Services:

Family courts should collaborate with social services, mental health professionals, and domestic violence advocates to provide comprehensive support to victims. This includes access to counseling, housing assistance, and legal aid.

## Child Custody Considerations:

Courts must consider the impact of domestic violence on children when making custody determinations. Presumptions of joint custody should be re-evaluated in cases involving domestic violence, and the safety and well-being of the child should be the primary concern.

**Accountability for Abusers**: Abusers must be held accountable for their actions. This includes ensuring that they comply with court orders, participate in intervention programs, and face appropriate legal consequences for their behavior.

# Conclusion

Jennifer's Law represents a crucial step forward in recognizing and addressing coercive control as a form of domestic violence. However, to truly protect victims and ensure justice, comprehensive family court reform is essential. By educating legal professionals, implementing protective measures, providing holistic support services, re-evaluating child custody considerations, and holding abusers accountable, we can create a legal system that better serves the needs of victims and their children. Only through these efforts can we hope to create a safer and more just society for all.

# CHAPTER 9: PERSONAL STORIES AND TESTIMONIALS

## Introduction

Personal stories and testimonials provide a human face to the issue of corruption in family courts. These accounts highlight the real-life impact of unjust rulings and unethical practices, offering a deeper understanding of the emotional, psychological, and financial toll on families. In this chapter, we share the experiences of several individuals who have navigated the challenging landscape of Connecticut's family court system.

# Emily's Story: A Battle for Custody

Emily, a mother of two, faced an uphill battle in her custody fight. Despite clear evidence of her ex-husband's abusive behavior, the court awarded him primary custody. Emily suspected that bribery was involved, as her ex-husband had connections within the legal community.

## The Impact

- **Emotional Toll:** Emily experienced severe anxiety and depression, feeling helpless as she watched her children suffer.
- **Financial Strain:** Legal fees drained her savings, forcing her to take on multiple jobs.
- **Ongoing Struggle:** Emily continues to fight for her children, seeking justice and a safe environment for them.

# Lisa's Story: Procedural Violations and Bias

Lisa, a professional woman, faced bias and procedural violations during her divorce proceedings. The court ignored key evidence of her ex-husband's infidelity and financial misconduct, leading to an unfair division of assets.

## The Impact

- **Career Disruption:** The prolonged legal battle affected Lisa's career, causing her to miss work and lose professional opportunities.
- **Emotional Distress:** The sense of injustice and ongoing legal challenges took a toll on Lisa's mental health.
- **Continued Fight:** Lisa remains determined to seek redress and expose the procedural violations that affected her case.

# David's Story: Guardians ad Litem and Conflict of Interest

David's case involved a guardian ad litem (GAL) who had a conflict of interest. The GAL's recommendations were heavily biased in favor of David's ex-wife, a personal friend, leading to an unfavorable custody arrangement.

## The Impact

- **Alienation:** David felt alienated from his children due to the biased recommendations and court rulings.
- **Financial Burden:** The cost of hiring multiple lawyers to challenge the GAL's recommendations drained David's finances.
- **Hope for Change:** David now advocates for greater oversight and accountability for GALs in family courts.

# Maria's Story: Fighting Bias and Prejudice

Maria, a minority woman, faced racial and socioeconomic bias in her custody case. Despite being a loving and capable mother, the court consistently ruled in favor of her ex-husband, who came from a more affluent background.

## The Impact

- **Emotional Trauma:** Maria struggled with feelings of inadequacy and despair, questioning her worth as a mother.
- **Community Support:** Through support groups and advocacy organizations, Maria found strength and solidarity.
- **Advocacy:** Maria now works with local advocacy groups to combat bias and promote fairness in family courts.

# Testimonials from Advocates
## Jane Doe, Family Court Reform Advocate

Jane Doe, a prominent advocate for family court reform, shares her insights on the systemic issues and the importance of continued advocacy.

- **Challenges:** Jane highlights the pervasive nature of corruption and the difficulties in bringing about change.
- **Success Stories:** Despite the challenges, Jane recounts instances where advocacy efforts led to positive outcomes and systemic reforms.
- **Call to Action:** Jane emphasizes the need for public support, legislative changes, and ongoing vigilance to protect families and ensure justice.

## John Smith, Legal Aid Attorney

John Smith, a legal aid attorney, provides a perspective on the legal challenges faced by families navigating the court system.

- **Legal Hurdles:** John discusses the procedural complexities and the impact of corruption on legal outcomes.
- **Support Systems:** He highlights the role of legal aid organizations in providing essential support to affected families.
- **Future Directions:** John advocates for increased funding for legal aid and stronger regulatory frameworks to prevent corruption.

# Conclusion

The personal stories and testimonials in this chapter illustrate the profound impact of corruption in Connecticut's family courts. These accounts underscore the urgent need for systemic reforms, greater accountability, and ongoing advocacy to protect families and ensure justice. By sharing these stories, we hope to raise awareness, inspire action, and contribute to the broader effort to create a fair and just family court system.

# Chapter 10: Reform Initiatives and Solutions

## Introduction

Addressing corruption in Connecticut's family courts requires comprehensive reform initiatives and practical solutions. This chapter outlines various strategies that can be implemented to improve transparency, accountability, and fairness within the family court system. By examining successful models from other jurisdictions and considering innovative approaches, we can chart a path toward a more just and equitable family court system in Connecticut.

# Enhancing Oversight and Accountability

## Judicial Review and Audits

Regular judicial reviews and audits are essential for ensuring that family court proceedings adhere to legal and ethical standards. Independent bodies should conduct these reviews to identify and address any instances of corruption or misconduct.

- **Example:** Establishing an independent judicial review board tasked with auditing family court cases annually.
- **Impact:** Increased accountability and transparency, leading to a reduction in corrupt practices and greater public trust in the judicial system.

# Strengthening Judicial Conduct Commissions

Judicial conduct commissions play a crucial role in investigating complaints against judges and court officials. Strengthening these commissions can enhance their ability to enforce ethical standards and hold corrupt officials accountable.

- **Example:** Expanding the powers of the Connecticut Judicial Review Council to impose stricter sanctions on judges found guilty of misconduct.
- **Impact:** Greater deterrence against unethical behavior and a more robust mechanism for addressing complaints and ensuring justice.

# Improving Training and Education

## Specialized Training for Family Court Judges

Family court judges should receive specialized training to handle the complexities of family law cases effectively. This training should cover topics such as child psychology, domestic violence, and the impact of bias and prejudice.

- **Example:** Implementing mandatory continuing education programs for family court judges focusing on family law and related areas.
- **Impact:** Better-informed judges capable of making fair and just decisions, reducing the likelihood of biased or uninformed rulings.

# Ethics Training for Court Officials

All court officials, including judges, lawyers, and guardians ad litem, should undergo regular ethics training to reinforce the importance of integrity and impartiality in the judicial process.

- **Example:** Developing a comprehensive ethics training curriculum for court officials, with periodic refresher courses.
- **Impact:** Enhanced awareness of ethical standards and a stronger commitment to upholding them, leading to more ethical behavior in family courts.

# Promoting Transparency

## Public Access to Court Records

Ensuring public access to court records can enhance transparency and allow for greater scrutiny of family court proceedings. This can help deter corrupt practices and provide a mechanism for the public to hold the court system accountable.

- **Example:** Creating an online database where court records and decisions are accessible to the public, with appropriate privacy safeguards.
- **Impact:** Increased transparency and accountability, enabling the public to monitor court activities and detect potential corruption.

## Transparent Appointment Processes

The appointment process for judges and guardians ad litem should be transparent and based on merit. Clear criteria and open selection procedures can help prevent favoritism and conflicts of interest.

- **Example:** Implementing a transparent and competitive

selection process for appointing judges and GALs, with public input and oversight.

- **Impact:** Reduced opportunities for corruption and increased public confidence in the impartiality and competence of court officials.

# Legislative and Policy Reforms

## Enacting Stronger Anti-Corruption Laws

Stronger anti-corruption laws can provide a legal framework for addressing and preventing corruption in family courts. These laws should include severe penalties for bribery, fraud, and other corrupt practices.

- **Example:** Passing legislation that increases penalties for bribery and fraud in family court cases and provides resources for investigating and prosecuting such crimes.

- **Impact:** A more robust legal deterrent against corruption, leading to a decrease in unethical behavior.

## Policy Reforms for Procedural Fairness

Policy reforms aimed at ensuring procedural fairness can help address systemic issues and prevent unjust outcomes. These reforms should focus on streamlining court processes, reducing delays, and ensuring equal treatment for all parties.

- **Example:** Implementing policies that require timely and fair hearings, equal access to legal resources, and consistent application of legal standards.
- **Impact:** More efficient and equitable court proceedings,

reducing opportunities for corruption and bias.

# Leveraging Technology
## Digital Case Management Systems

Adopting digital case management systems can improve the efficiency and transparency of family court proceedings. These systems can streamline case handling, reduce administrative errors, and provide real-time access to case information.

- **Example:** Implementing an integrated digital case management system for all family court cases in Connecticut.
- **Impact:** Increased efficiency, reduced administrative burdens, and enhanced transparency, leading to fairer and more timely outcomes.

# Online Dispute Resolution

Online dispute resolution (ODR) platforms can provide an alternative to traditional court proceedings, offering a more accessible and efficient way to resolve family law disputes. ODR can help reduce the caseload of family courts and provide a less adversarial environment for resolving conflicts.

- **Example:** Developing an ODR platform for family law cases, allowing parties to mediate and resolve disputes online.
- **Impact:** Reduced court caseloads, quicker resolutions, and a more user-friendly process for families.

# Community and Stakeholder Involvement

## Engaging Community Organizations

Community organizations play a vital role in supporting families and advocating for reforms. Engaging these organizations in the reform process can provide valuable insights and resources.

- **Example:** Forming partnerships between family courts and community organizations to provide support services and advocate for policy changes.
- **Impact:** Enhanced support for families and a stronger, community-driven push for systemic reforms.

## Stakeholder Collaboration

Collaboration among stakeholders, including judges, lawyers, advocacy groups, and policymakers, is essential for driving meaningful reforms. Regular dialogue and cooperation can help identify issues, develop solutions, and ensure effective implementation of reforms.

- **Example:** Establishing a family court reform task force comprising representatives from various stakeholder groups to develop and monitor reform initiatives.
- **Impact:** More coordinated and effective reform efforts, leading to a fairer and more transparent family court system.

## Conclusion

Reforming Connecticut's family court system to address corruption requires a multifaceted approach that includes enhancing oversight and accountability, improving training and education, promoting transparency, enacting legislative and policy reforms, leveraging technology, and involving the community and stakeholders. By implementing these strategies, we can create a family court system that upholds the principles of justice, fairness, and integrity, ensuring that all families receive fair treatment and that corrupt practices are eradicated. Through these collective efforts, we can build a judicial system that truly serves the best interests of families in Connecticut.

# CONCLUSION

## Recap of Key Issues

The corruption within Connecticut's family court system has profound and far-reaching consequences, affecting countless families and undermining public trust in the judicial system. Throughout this book, we have examined various aspects of this corruption, including systemic issues, legal and ethical violations, and the personal stories of those impacted. The experiences of individuals like Emily, Michael, Lisa, David, and Maria illustrate the devastating emotional, financial, and psychological toll of corrupt practices and biased rulings.

## The Importance of Advocacy and Reform

Addressing these issues requires the concerted efforts of advocacy groups, legal professionals, policymakers, and the public. Advocacy plays a vital role in raising awareness, supporting affected families, and pushing for necessary reforms. Organizations such as the Connecticut Coalition for Family Court Reform and the National Family Court Watch Project provide critical support and drive change through their tireless work.

## Proposed Solutions

Reforming Connecticut's family courts involves a comprehensive approach that includes:

- **Enhancing Oversight and Accountability:** Regular audits, independent review boards, and strengthened judicial conduct commissions are essential for maintaining transparency and deterring corrupt practices.
- **Improving Training and Education:** Specialized training

for judges and ethics training for all court officials can help ensure fair and informed decision-making.

- **Promoting Transparency:** Public access to court records and transparent appointment processes are crucial for preventing favoritism and conflicts of interest.
- **Legislative and Policy Reforms:** Stronger anti-corruption laws, procedural fairness policies, and policy reforms can create a more equitable legal framework.
- **Leveraging Technology:** Digital case management systems and online dispute resolution platforms can enhance efficiency and accessibility.
- **Community and Stakeholder Involvement:** Engaging community organizations and fostering stakeholder

collaboration can provide valuable insights and support for reform initiatives.

## Moving Forward

The path to reform is challenging, but it is essential for restoring integrity and fairness in Connecticut's family courts. By implementing the solutions discussed in this book and fostering a culture of accountability and transparency, we can work towards a judicial system that truly serves the best interests of all families.

## A Call to Action

Change cannot happen without the collective effort of individuals, communities, and institutions. Whether you are a legal professional, an advocate, a policymaker, or a concerned citizen, your role in this fight is crucial. Advocate for legislative changes, support organizations that provide resources and assistance to affected families, and demand transparency and accountability from the judicial system.

## Final Thoughts

The stories and insights shared in this book underscore the urgent need for reform in Connecticut's family courts. By addressing corruption head-on and implementing meaningful changes, we can ensure that justice is served and that all families are treated with the fairness and respect they deserve. Together, we can build a judicial system that upholds the highest standards of integrity and works in the best interests of all its constituents.

# APPENDICES

## Appendix A: Resources for Affected Families

### Legal Assistance

1. Connecticut Legal Services (CLS)
   - Website: www.connlegalservices.org
   - Services: Provides free legal assistance to low-income individuals in civil matters, including family law.
2. Greater Hartford Legal Aid (GHLA)
   - Website: www.ghla.org
   - Services: Offers legal help in family law cases, including custody, child support, and protection from abuse.

3. Statewide Legal Services of Connecticut (SLS)
   - ○ Website: www.slsct.org
   - ○ Services: Provides free legal advice and referrals for low-income residents of Connecticut.

# Advocacy and Support Organizations

1. Connecticut Coalition for Family Court Reform (CCFCR)
   - ○ Website: www.ccfcr.org
   - ○ Mission: Advocates for reforms in the family court system and provides support to affected families.
2. National Family Court Watch Project (NFCWP)
   - ○ Website: www.nfcwp.org
   - ○ Mission: Monitors family court proceedings and advocates for systemic reforms.

3. Parents' Rights in Action (PRA)
   - ○ Website:
     www.parentsrights.org
   - ○ Mission: Supports parents
     navigating the family
     court system and
     advocates for their rights.

# Counseling and Emotional Support

1. Family ReEntry
   - ○ Website:
     www.familyreentry.org
   - ○ Services: Provides
     counseling and support
     services for families
     dealing with court-related
     stress.
2. The Center for Family Justice
   - ○ Website:
     www.centerforfamilyjustic
     e.org
   - ○ Services: Offers crisis
     counseling, support
     groups, and legal

advocacy for victims of
domestic violence.
3. Connecticut Alliance to End
Sexual Violence
   o Website:
     www.endsexualviolencect.
     org
   o Services: Provides
     counseling and advocacy
     for survivors of sexual
     violence and their families.

# Appendix B: Glossary of Terms

## Legal Terms

1. Bribery
   - Definition: The offering, giving, receiving, or soliciting of something of value to influence the actions of an official.
2. Conflict of Interest
   - Definition: A situation in which a person or organization has competing interests or loyalties.
3. Guardian ad Litem (GAL)
   - Definition: A court-appointed advocate for a child in a legal case, responsible for representing the child's best interests.
4. Judicial Conduct Commission

- o Definition: An independent body that investigates complaints against judges and enforces ethical standards.
5. Procedural Fairness
   - o Definition: The requirement that legal proceedings be conducted in a fair and impartial manner, following established rules and protocols.

## Advocacy Terms

1. Advocacy
   - o Definition: The act or process of supporting a cause or proposal to influence public policy and resource allocation decisions.
2. Transparency
   - o Definition: Openness, accountability, and

straightforwardness in the conduct of business and decision-making processes.

3. Oversight
   - Definition: The process of monitoring and regulating the activities of organizations and individuals to ensure compliance with laws and standards.

# Appendix C: Legislative and Policy Recommendations

## Legislative Proposals

1. Anti-Corruption Legislation
   - Proposal: Enact laws that increase penalties for bribery, fraud, and other corrupt practices in family court cases.
   - Impact: Provide a stronger deterrent against unethical behavior and enhance the legal framework for prosecuting corruption.
2. Judicial Review Board
   - Proposal: Establish an independent board to conduct regular audits and reviews of family court proceedings.
   - Impact: Increase accountability and

transparency in the family court system.

3. Conflict of Interest Guidelines
   - Proposal: Implement clear guidelines and disclosure requirements for judges, lawyers, and court officials to prevent conflicts of interest.
   - Impact: Reduce opportunities for favoritism and ensure impartial decision-making.

## Policy Reforms

1. Equal Representation Policies
   - Proposal: Ensure equal access to legal representation for all parties in family court cases, regardless of financial status.
   - Impact: Level the playing field and promote fairer outcomes.

2. Ethics Training Programs
    o Proposal: Develop mandatory ethics training programs for all court officials, with periodic refresher courses.
    o Impact: Reinforce ethical standards and reduce instances of unethical behavior.
3. Public Access to Court Records
    o Proposal: Create an online database for public access to court records, with appropriate privacy safeguards.
    o Impact: Enhance transparency and enable public monitoring of court activities.

# Appendix D: Further Reading and References

## Books and Articles

1.  "The Divorce Culture" by Barbara Dafoe Whitehead
    o   Description: Examines the social and cultural changes that have influenced divorce and family law.
2.  "Taken Into Custody: The War Against Fathers, Marriage, and the Family" by Stephen Baskerville
    o   Description: Explores issues within the family court system, particularly focusing on biases against fathers.
3.  "The War on Kids: How American Juvenile Justice Lost Its Way" by Cara H. Drinan

- o Description: Provides an in-depth look at the challenges within the juvenile justice system, relevant to family court issues.

## Reports and Studies

1. "State of Connecticut Judicial Branch Annual Report"
   - o Description: Provides insights into the operations, challenges, and achievements of the Connecticut Judicial Branch.
   - o Availability: www.jud.ct.gov
2. "National Family Court Watch Project Annual Report"
   - o Description: Offers data and analysis on family court proceedings across the United States.

o   Availability:
    www.nfcwp.org
3. "Reforming Family Justice: A
   Pathway to Progress"
    o   Description: A
        comprehensive report
        outlining
        recommendations for
        improving the family
        court system.
    o   Availability: Various legal
        and advocacy
        organizations' websites.

## Conclusion

These appendices provide valuable
resources, definitions, legislative
proposals, policy recommendations, and
further reading materials to help
individuals understand and address the
issues of corruption in Connecticut's
family courts. By leveraging these
resources, advocating for necessary
reforms, and staying informed, we can

work collectively towards a more just and equitable family court system.